ALL SCALES IN ALL POSITIONS FOR GUITAR

by Muriel Anderson
and Jim Scott

Featuring Jim Scott's revolutionary "rows" concept

*This book is dedicated to our students, comrades, and teachers—
and to those who fall into all three categories.
Special thanks to Matt Donovan and Fritzi Scott,
for their support and inspiration.*

See page 71 for MOVEABLE SCALE FINDER

ISBN 978-0-634-01049-1

HAL•LEONARD®
C O R P O R A T I O N
7777 W. BLUEMOUND RD. P.O. BOX 13819 MILWAUKEE, WI 53213

Visit Hal Leonard Online at
www.halleonard.com

INTRODUCTION

This book is designed to help you discover and recognize the patterns that make up many types of scales. Uncovering the secrets of scale construction can give you a better handle on spontaneous improvisation and creating melodies. By exploring scale patterns from several different angles, you will develop the ability to let the notes fall underneath your fingers, moving seamlessly from one position to the next.

We'll start off with the major scale—how it's constructed, how to visualize it on a single string and then the entire fretboard, and how to come up with usable patterns. The core of our exploration will be a concept called **rows**—a unique way of looking at scales *across* the neck that will help you in developing fingerings and in memorizing and transposing scales.

After the major scale, we'll look at other scale types—pentatonic, blues, natural minor, harmonic minor, melodic minor, whole tone, diminished, chromatic—and the modes.

Along the way, we'll explore a number of practice techniques, including sequential fingerings, the circle of fifths, and improvisation using chord-scales and motifs. We'll even go off the beaten path to touch on harp-style fingerings and alternate tunings.

Good luck!

—Jim Scott & Muriel Anderson

CONTENTS

THE MAJOR SCALE

A *scale* is a series of notes arranged in order; a selection of pitches that can be used to create melodies. First, let's define the major, or "diatonic" scale. In all, the major scale contains seven different notes. You can also see it as a series of whole steps (the distance of two frets) and half steps (the distance of one fret). The intervallic formula for constructing the major scale is as follows: whole–whole–half–whole–whole–whole–half. Each fret is the equivalent of one half step, so in frets that translates to: 2–2–1–2–2–2–1.

Fig. 1A Major Scale Formula

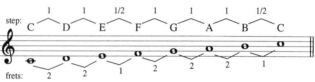

You can think of this as two groups of whole– whole–half (2–2–1), separated by a whole step. (By the way, these four-note groups are called *tetrachords.* So the scale is made up of two tetrachords, separated by a whole step.)

VISUALIZING THE MAJOR SCALE ON ONE STRING

Using the major scale formula above, it is possible to hlocate all of the notes of the major scale on one string. If you begin on the first fret of the first string (an F note), the result is an F major scale.

Fig. 1B: Major Scale Formula

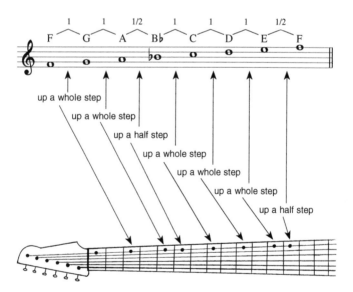

The notes of the F major scale end up on frets 1, 3, 5, 6, 8, 10, 12, and 13. You can recognize this as a pattern. The first three frets are odd numbers, and the next four are even numbers (until you return to the root again on the thirteenth fret).

Think about that for a moment; for any major scale on one string that starts on an odd-numbered fret, the notes of the scale will land on three odd-numbered frets and then four even-numbered frets. For any major scale that starts on an even-numbered fret, the scale will start with three even-numbered frets and then land on four odd numbers. Try this starting on any note, saying the fret numbers aloud. This information will come in handy later when analyzing and remembering scale positions.

VISUALIZING THE MAJOR SCALE ON TWO STRINGS

Fill in the notes of the F major scale on the second string. Then, look at the notes lining up on the first and second strings. On frets 1, 3, 5, 6, 8, and 10 are two notes straight across from each other (the interval of a perfect fourth). The first and second strings are tuned a perfect fourth apart, as is most of the guitar (with the exception of the interval between the second and third strings, which is a major third). Perfect fourths occur between many notes of the scale, as is evidenced by the six "straight rows" you see here. The one row that forms a diagonal (second string, eleventh fret and first string, twelfth fret) is an augmented fourth.

Fig. 2: F Major Scale (Top Two Strings)

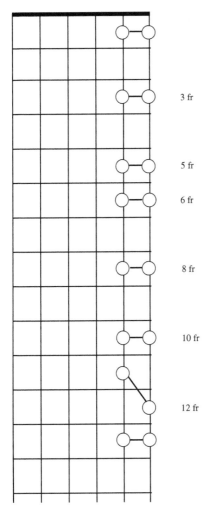

Exercise:
Improvise using the F major scale over an F major chord or a D minor chord.

HAND POSITION

Place your hand in one position on the guitar neck, assigning one finger to each fret. If your fingers are on frets 1, 2, 3, and 4, this is called "first position." If your fingers are on frets 2, 3, 4, and 5, this is called "second position," etc.

Fig. 3: Finger Position

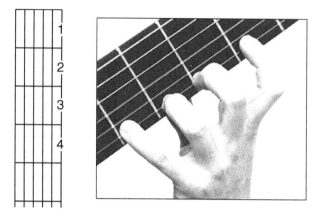

In one position, you can typically find three notes of a scale on a single string. Use the finger assigned to each fret; if the notes go up a whole step (two frets), leave out one finger. You may need to reach an extra fret with the first or fourth finger.

Fig. 4: Hand Position (One String)

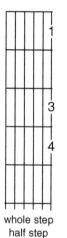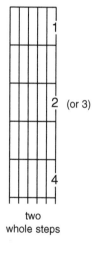

whole step half step   half step whole step   two whole steps

SIX-NOTE BLOCKS

If you play three notes per position on each of the two strings, you have a six-note block in any position. Aha! Six notes to create melodies or to improvise on the scale in seven positions! And looking ahead, you can find six-note blocks with any two adjacent strings tuned a perfect fourth apart (i.e., except between the second and third strings).

Fig. 5: Adjacent String Blocks

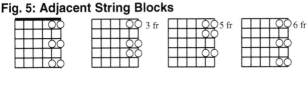

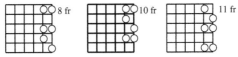

LOCATING NOTES ON THE SIXTH STRING

This part is easy. You already know that the sixth string contains the same notes as the first string, two octaves below.

Fig. 6: F Major Scale, Strings 1, 2, and 6

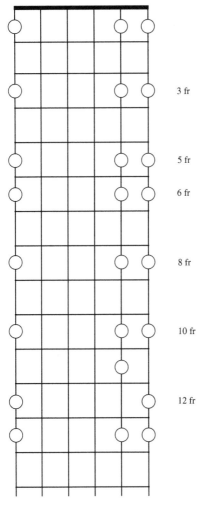

Exercise:
Try improvising with a friend, one playing the bass notes up and down the sixth string, and the other playing melody notes on the first and second strings.

7

SEVEN "ROWS" OF NOTES

Notice in the previous diagram that you can see rows of notes emerging across the fingerboard. Here is the quantum leap! The following is a diagram of the F major scale on all the strings across the entire fingerboard. We have selected the F major scale as an example simply because the first row of this scale starts right on the first fret. You can move this "map" to create any major scale simply by beginning on another fret. More about this later...

Fig. 7: F Major Scale, All Six Strings

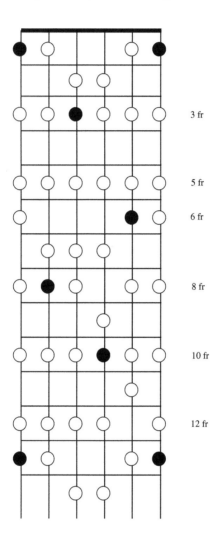

At first glance, the diagram may look as complicated as a chessboard...How to remember all of these notes?

Well, you may notice that some notes form straight lines across the fingerboard. Looking further, we can see other notes falling into "crooked rows" between no more than two frets across the fingerboard. We have already discovered that notes on the first and sixth strings are the same. Now, let's "connect the dots" into seven rows, like this:

Fig. 8: Visualizing the Rows

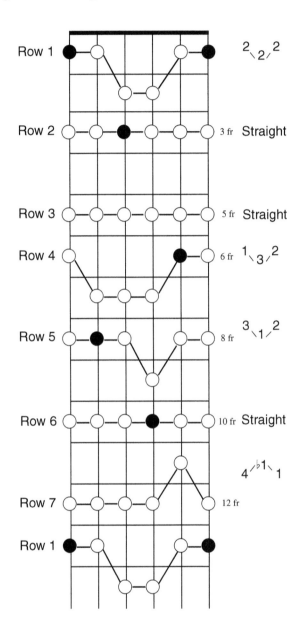

NOTE:
The major scale and its *relative minor* scale contain the same notes. The relative minor starts on the sixth step of the major scale. Every major scale diagram in this book is also a diagram of a natural minor scale. Therefore, you can see that the diagram above represents both the F major (beginning on an F note) and D minor scales (beginning on a D note).

HOW TO READ THE ROWS

To describe the first row we might say, "Two notes on first fret of the sixth and fifth strings, then up one fret two notes on the fourth and third strings, then back to first fret, two notes, second and first strings." But that's too confusing! To abbreviate this, we will simply call this row "2–2–2," symbolizing the pattern. All row names follow this system:

- The first number refers to how many notes appear straight across the same fret (before moving up or down one fret).
- The second number refers to how many notes appear straight across the next fret.
- The third number refers to how many notes appear straight across the fret (after moving back to the original fret).

To recap, we presume the second number denotes a move up one fret unless indicated by "♭" to mean that the row moves back one fret. This will start to make more sense as you begin working with and seeing the shapes of the rows.

Fig. 9: Sample Row

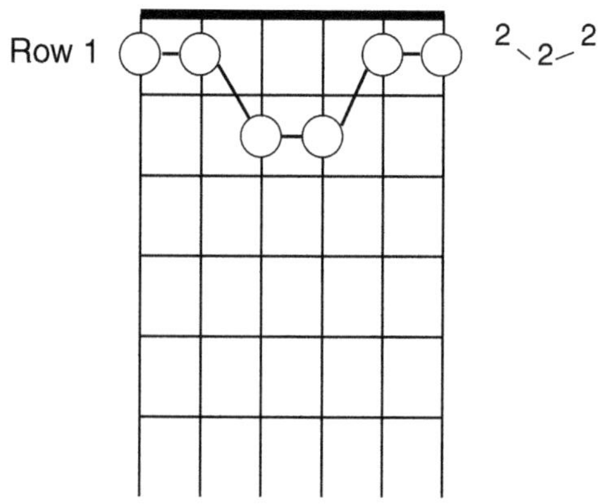

These lines of notes, or rows as we will refer to them, are comprised of notes of the scale you just happen to find as you go across the fingerboard. We number these rows according to the scale degree that is on either end of the row. The first row has the first scale degree (or root, in this case the F note) on either end (both the top and bottom string). There is one row for each of the seven notes of the scale.

Eventually, we will find that these rows will have some applications to chords as well as scales and modes. But more of that later...

For now, what is the point of this visual map? First of all, any three consecutive rows make a scale fingering.

EXTRACTING SCALES

Let's look at rows 1, 2, and 3. As you play across the fingerboard, three notes per string, you will find this gives you a complete major scale with one slight problem: the third note on the third string and the first note on the second string are the same note. This happens in every position (with every three consecutive rows). Why? Since most of the guitar is tuned in fourths, we typically play three notes per string before moving to the next string. However, since the second and third strings are tuned a third apart, we can only fit in two notes on the third or second string without duplicating a note. You can decide which of the notes to leave out, depending on which string is more convenient to your hand position.

Fig. 10A: Major Scale Pattern

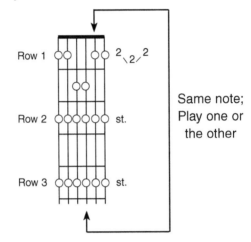

Same note;
Play one or
the other

Here are two ways to play this scale in one position. The numbers refer to the left-hand fingerings.

Fig. 10B: Major Scale Fingerings

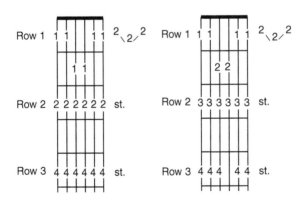

We start here because the scale begins on the *root* of the scale. These fingerings, however, span five frets in the first and second positions where the frets are wide, and as a result, they require the biggest stretches. Let's try two other positions that encompass only four frets.

COMPACT SCALE PATTERNS

Compact scale patterns that span only four frets are typically the best patterns to begin with. First, extract rows 3, 4, and 5. This scale pattern spans only four frets, allowing you to assign one finger per fret. The numbers in circles are the root, or first degree, of the scale. To get the sound of the major scale in your ears, move up and down the scale beginning and ending with the circled note. Notice that this diagram begins with the third note of the scale as the lowest note. (If you started and ended with the lowest note in this position, this would be called a Phrygian scale. See p. 37). In this fingering, we leave out the highest note on the third string since it would involve an extension of the fourth finger.

Practicing playing this pattern in different positions up and down the neck:

Fig. 11A: Another Major Scale Pattern

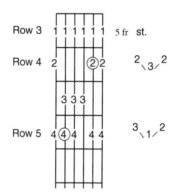

Now, extract rows 7, 1, and 2. The notes in circles are the root of the scale. Move up and down the scale beginning and ending with the root. Notice that this diagram begins with the seventh note of the scale as the lowest note. Once again, we have a duplicate note on the second and third strings. The easiest way to finger this scale is to play three notes on the third string and two on the second string. Play this in any position:

Fig. 11B: Yet Another Major Scale Pattern

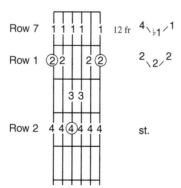

MAJOR SCALE FINGERINGS

Here are the seven patterns for an F major scale (with the root circled) in each position beginning with successive notes of the scale. The numbers refer to the left-hand fingerings. Play the scale in seven positions, noting where the circled root (in this case, F) lies. Alternate fingerings are given on the following page. To get the sound of the scale in your ears, practice beginning and ending the scale with one of the circled notes.

Fig. 12: Major Scale, Seven Different Patterns

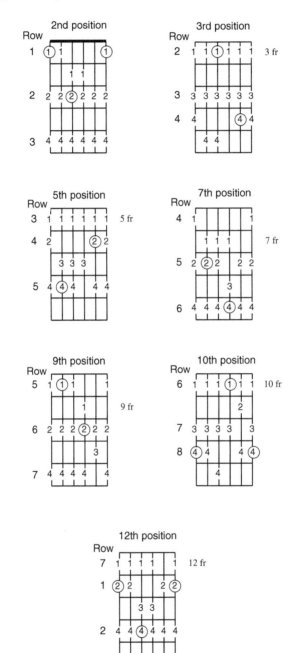

NOTE:

The first and fourth fingers can stretch one fret when necessary, so technically the positions are determined by the second and third fingers, which always stay on the same frets. Also, notice that in each pattern, there is always one note left out of the three full rows.

Now, let's take a look at alternate fingerings for five of the scales shown above. With these, you'll now have a total of twelve fingerings, making it possible to play the F major scale in all twelve positions on the fretboard. You can also play these twelve scale fingerings in one position—one for each of the 12 keys.

Fig. 13: Major Scales, Five Alternate Patterns

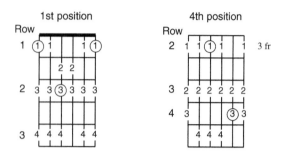

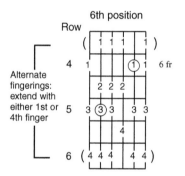

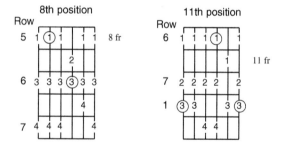

SCALES WITHOUT STRETCHES

On the next page is a set of five scale fingerings that cover the entire fingerboard without any extended reaches. Three of the fingerings shift down to notes from the previous row, rather than extending up. The other two scales have no extensions. The *Aaron Shearer Method,* a widely used classical guitar series, uses this system of scales exclusively, and some guitarists play entirely with this system.

Fig. 14: Major Scales, No Stretches

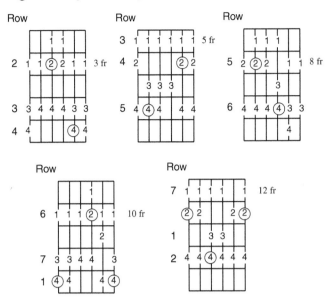

OPEN-POSITION SCALES

Here are patterns that incorporate open strings. Notice the rows within these patterns. The B♭ scale borrows a note from an adjacent row. Assign your index finger to the first fret, your middle finger to the second fret, your ring finger to the third fret, and your little finger to the fourth fret. Note the relationship of the chord shapes to the scale patterns.

Fig. 15: Major Scales in Open Position

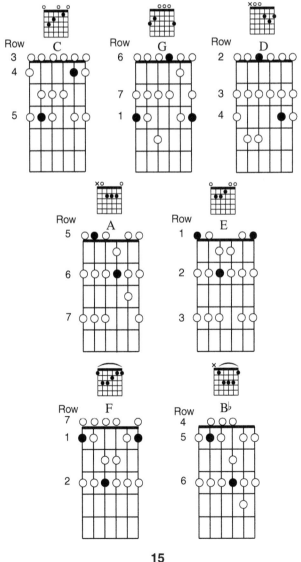

TRANSPOSING SCALES

All scale patterns are moveable. The circled note (the root, or first degree of the scale) is the name of the scale. Open strings are considered fret "0" and must be moved up just like positions on the other frets. For example, to construct the C major scale, all the rows move up seven frets. The seven rows repeat themselves in the next octave, so you can think of the pattern as extending infinitely in either direction. To help visualize this, see the moveable scale guide at the back of the book on page 71.

Fig. 16: Comparing Major Scale Patterns

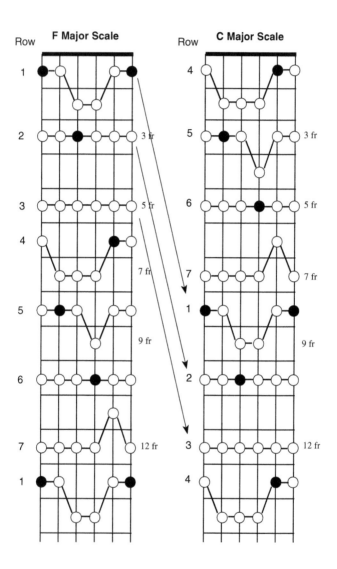

SHIFTING FROM ONE POSITION TO ANOTHER

Here are three ways to move from one position to the next. The numbers on the fingerboard indicate left-hand fingering.

Fig. 17A: Play One Note and Shift

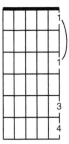
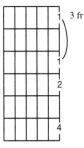
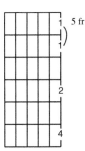

Fig. 17B: Play Two Notes and Shift

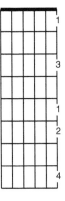
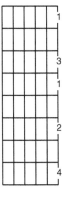

Fig. 17C: Play Three Notes and Shift

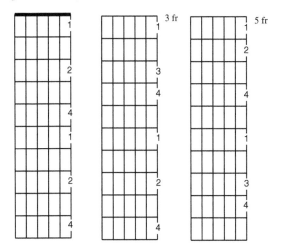

Sometimes you may find it convenient to shift with the fourth finger, especially when descending.

Fig. 17D: Another Option

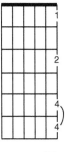

Here are several scales using the three types of shifts mentioned on the previous page. These are just a few examples. Practice shifting from any step of the scale on any string. When you play one-note-and-shift, you move up one row. When you play two-notes-and-shift, you move up two rows. When you play three-notes-and-shift, you move up three rows. Try each key, reading down one column.

Fig. 18A: One Note and Shift

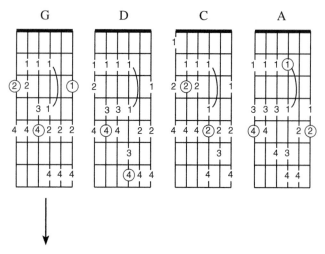

Fig. 18B: Two Notes and Shift

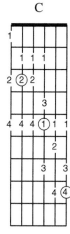
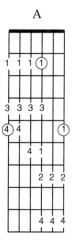

Fig. 18C: Three Notes and Shift

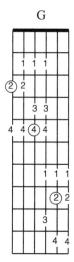
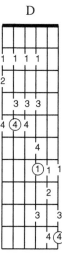
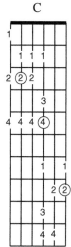
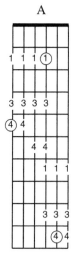

These next examples shift on the fourth string instead of on the third.

Fig. 18D: One Note and Shift

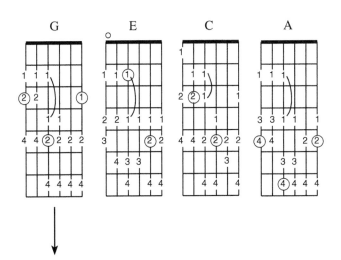

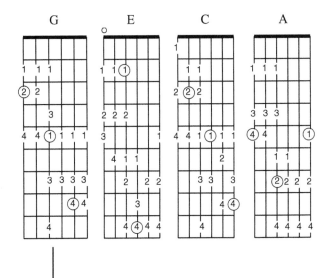

Fig. 18E: Two Notes and Shift

Fig. 18F: Three Notes and Shift

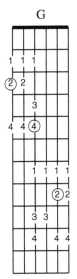
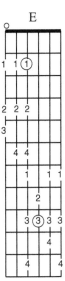
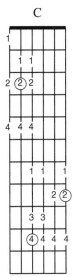
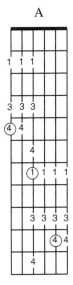

THREE-NOTES-PER-STRING SCALES

Playing three notes per string will move you up (at the second string) to the next position as you ascend. Try this in all seven positions, beginning with any note of the scale. This is a great way to play scales fast, especially if you use hammer-ons when ascending and pull-offs when descending. Many rock players use this method extensively.

Fig. 19: Major Scales, Three Notes Per String

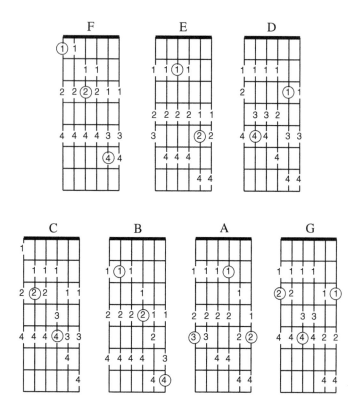

TWO-NOTES-PER-STRING SCALES

Playing two notes per string will move you backward along the fingerboard.

Fig. 20A: Major Scales, Two Notes Per String

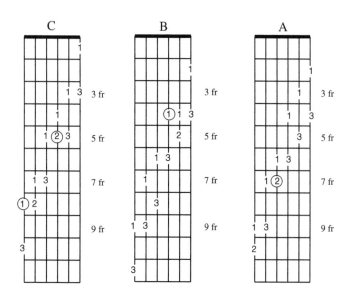

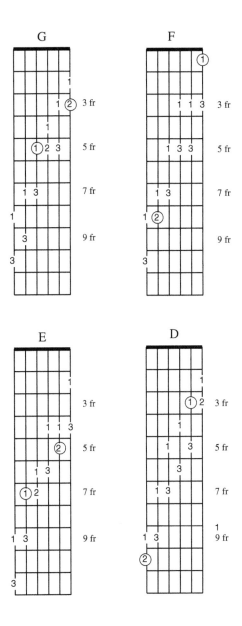

This involves a great deal of shifting but may come in handy when phrasing patterns like the following:

Fig. 20B: Position-Shifting Phrase #1

Fig. 20C: Position-Shifting Phrase #2

CHORDS WITHIN SCALES

The example given below is based on the C major scale—but the patterns follow the same order for all major scales. If you circle the first, third, and fifth notes (scale degrees) of the C major scale everywhere up and down the fingerboard, you will have a diagram of every C major chord, everywhere on the fingerboard. This is the "I" chord ("one," or tonic chord) for the scale. (For further exploration, refer to the book *All Chords in All Positions*.) Notice where these chords fall in relation to the scale rows. The chord forms may help you to remember the row positions. They also outline the root and important notes in the scale. We can label each scale position (each set of three consecutive rows) by the tonic chord shape that falls within its range. We identify these by the familiar first-position chord shapes that would occur if you put a capo across the beginning of each row. These shapes fall exactly in reverse-alphabetical order as you move up the fingerboard.

Remember that these are simply terms we are giving to the shapes to help us to remember them—all the shapes are still C chords, derived from the C scale.

NOTE:
The numbers on this diagram refer to scale degrees.

Fig. 21: C Major Chords Inside C Major Scale

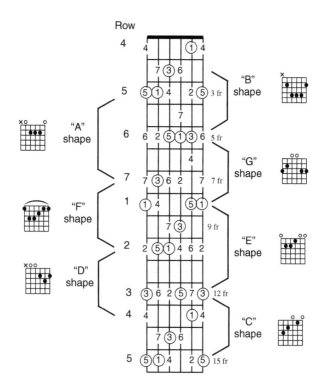

FINDING THE I, IV, AND V CHORDS

The diagram below shows the three basic chords in any scale: the I, IV, and V chords. In the key of C, this would be C, F, and G. Included is every note that you could play on each string.

Fig. 22A: Primary Chords, Key of C

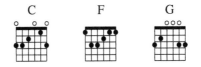

Now, let's put all three diagrams on the same grid. Cumulatively, all of the notes of the scale are contained in these three chords. So, the result is the C major scale.

Fig. 22B: Primary Chords Combined, Key of C

Conversely, within every scale position you can find every chord that occurs naturally within the scale.

THE GUITAR'S TUNING SYSTEM

The current tuning system for the guitar (low to high), E–A–D–G–B–E, has evolved to accommodate the formation of chords. The strings are tuned in fourths, with the exception of the interval between the second and third strings, which is a major third. This adjustment allows for an even two-octave interval between the first and sixth strings, greatly facilitating the use of the guitar as an accompaniment instrument. However, this also requires an adjustment of interval shapes between strings, as the patterns of the intervals are shifted one fret between the second and third strings. Some guitarists, like Stanley Jordan, who use the guitar primarily as a melody instrument, have chosen to tune the strings entirely in fourths, which makes it possible to keep the same fingering patterns across all six strings (see page 68).

TRIADS WITHIN THE SCALE ROWS

Looking at the top three strings, you can see familiar three-note chords (called *triads*) within each row. Extracting these triads will give you the chords that occur naturally on each step of the scale—the "harmonized scale"! Below is an example of the F major scale harmonized with triads.

Fig. 23: Triads Within the F Major Scale

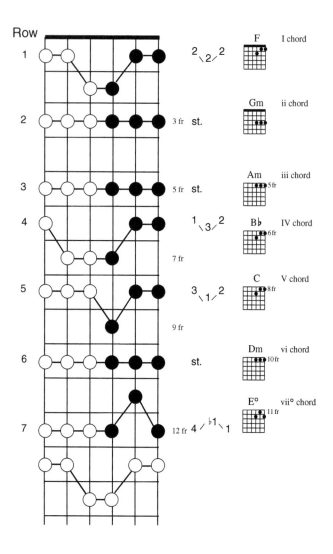

Find these triads for yourself on the second, third, and fourth strings.

SEVENTH CHORDS WITHIN THE SCALE ROWS

Within the rows, we can also find the seventh chords that occur naturally within the scale (again, called the "harmonized scale"). These are all in "root position," meaning they have the root of the chord in the bass.

Fig. 24: Seventh Chords Within the F Major Scale

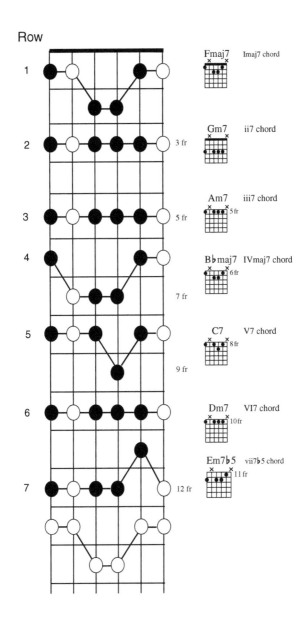

These are typical jazz voicings, played only on strings 6, 4, 3, and 2. To be able to strum the chord in addition to picking individual notes, the left-hand finger that plays the sixth string touches the fifth string just enough to deaden it, and likewise the first string is also deadened. The top four strings will yield another inversion of the same chords, (substituting notes on the first string for notes on the sixth).

PRACTICING SCALES

Great playing is first and foremost about having great tone. So, the very first step in developing good technique is to listen to the tone of each individual note. Practicing for speed is useless if the basic sound coming out of your instrument is like chalk against a blackboard. Listen carefully to hear that each note is clear, and take care to keep from chopping off the notes. Work to minimize extraneous noises. Think of tone as "the Holy Grail."

RIGHT-HAND TECHNIQUE

Scales can be used to improve your right-hand technique in general. Here are some suggestions to work on, whether you are playing with your fingers or a pick:

Fingerstyle

Position your hand so that your fingers are hanging over a given string, at a relaxed angle (fingers almost straight, perpendicular to the string). Play each note very slowly, alternating the index and middle fingers, watching the hand to be sure that each finger falls back to position after each stroke. Your fingers will only fall back to position if your hand is relaxed. If your hand is tense, it will take an extra motion to pull the finger back to position. Each stroke moves mostly from the big knuckle, stroking across the string instead of plucking up into the palm of the hand, allowing only a very slight bend (at most) in the first two joints. Each stroke needs to strike across the string quickly, without allowing the finger to rest on the string. This will allow the notes to ring longer and reduce separation between notes. Very slow and concentrated practice on hand relaxation between notes can work to eventually greatly improve the speed and fluidity of your music. Try this also with other sets of fingers: middle and ring, index and ring, thumb and index.

Playing with a Pick

Relax the hand so that there is just enough tension to hold the pick. Don't worry if it drops out of your hand a couple of times while you are finding that balancing point. An angle slightly at a diagonal to the string decreases resistance and will make the notes come out fatter and cleaner. Straight-up-and-down makes the pick sounds more audible. Alternate with down/up strokes. Then play the scale reversed, with up/down strokes. This makes for very rhythmic playing. At high speeds with a more legato sound, try using two downstrokes or two upstrokes when going from one string to the next.

SCALE EXERCISES

In playing music, you very rarely play an entire scale up and down. Instead, you might play melodies that contain both skips and consecutive notes. So, it would be good practice to play all of your scales in various ways, to attain flexibility using the scale. Practice going up the scale, then turning around and going back down randomly, developing the ability to change directions at any point.

Here are two patterns: one incorporating skips of thirds, and another that incorporates a three-note sequence. You can use these patterns with any scale in any position.

Fig. 25A: C Major Scale, in Thirds

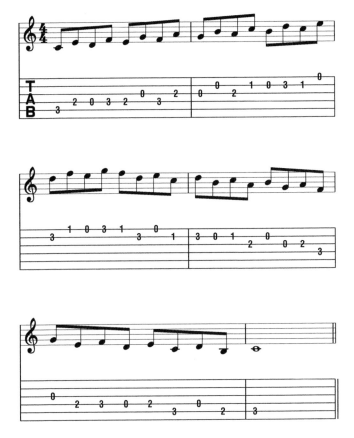

Fig. 25B: C Major Scale, Three-Note Sequence

DOTTED PATTERNS

This is the single best exercise to develop speed. By breaking up the scales to "long-short" and then "short-long," you are playing every other note as quickly and cleanly as possible, yet giving yourself time to think and listen to the sound of each note. It is important to work on both patterns—be sure to practice developing a quick finger motion between each pair of fingers. In the first exercise, try to make the time between the second and third notes as short as possible, while you can take as long as you like between the first and second notes.

Fig. 26A: "Long-Short" Rhythmic Pattern

Then, reverse the pattern. Try to make the time between the first and second notes as short as possible.

Fig. 26B: "Short-Long" Rhythmic Pattern

ACCENTS

It is important to have control of the volume of all the notes of the scale. Practice accenting every third note. Use a metronome to be sure that all the notes are at the same tempo. To really take control of your scales, practice accenting every fourth note, then every fifth note, every sixth note, and finally, every seventh note. You will find your speed improving when you concentrate your efforts on groups of notes in this way.

Fig. 27A: C Major Scale, with Accents

You also might play two notes of the scale at once. For example, play up the scale in thirds:

Fig. 27B: F Major Scale, in Thirds

Or, try playing up the scale in sixths:

Fig. 27C: F Major Scale, in Sixths

Try also playing closed-position fingerings in thirds and sixths. Then, try harmonizing the scale in tenths, fourths and fifths.

*P*entatonic scales are a five-note scales, universal to music around the world. ("Penta" means five.) Leaving out the fourth and seventh steps of the major scale will give us the scale most often referred to as the *major pentatonic scale.* We number the scale degrees as 1, 2, 3, 5, and 6, referring back to the notes of the major scale from which they were derived. We label the rows the same way, leaving out rows 4 and 7.

Fig. 28: C Major Pentatonic Scale

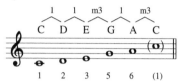

Thus, the major pentatonic scale is composed: whole step, whole step, minor third, whole step, minor third.

Here is the C major pentatonic scale diagrammed over the entire fingerboard.

Fig. 29: C Major Pentatonic Scale,
Across Entire Fingerboard

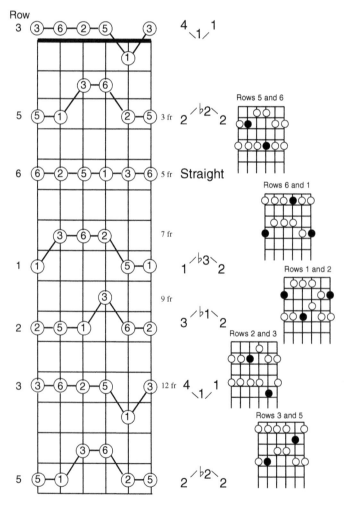

The beauty of the major pentatonic scale is that any two consecutive rows make a major pentatonic scale fingering. There are five notes in the major pentatonic scale, so there are five rows.

RELATING THE PENTATONIC SCALE TO THE MAJOR SCALE

You can practice a regular major scale, taking care to leave out the fourth and seventh scale degrees. This is a great way to attain the flexibility of moving back and forth from major to major pentatonic. Technically, it should be possible to play the major pentatonic scale in any of the seven positions of the major scale, even though two of the notes of the scale are left out.

Fig. 30: Finding C Major Pentatonic in a C Major Scale

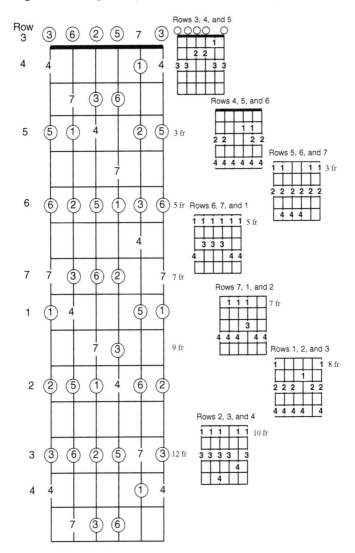

You can also think of the major pentatonic scale as a minor pentatonic scale by beginning on the sixth (A in the key of C). This works because the natural minor scale is the same as the major scale, but starting on the sixth degree of the scale (also called the "Aeolian mode.") In rock, blues, and pop music, the pentatonic scale is often played with the sixth as the root.

Take a moment to compare the rows of the major scale (or its relative minor) with the rows of the major pentatonic scale. Rows 4 and 7 have been omitted from the major pentatonic scale diagram.

Fig. 31: Comparing the "Rows"

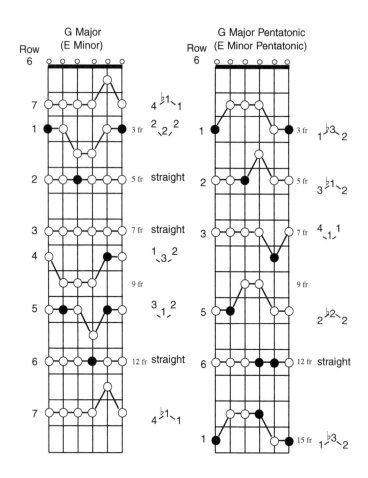

Play this major pentatonic scale against these progressions. Notice that the same scale works against all of these chords.

Fig. 32 Sample Chord Progressions
(for G Major or E Minor Pentatonic)

*Using the "minor pentatonic" scale (i.e., starting on the sixth degree of the major pentatonic scale) against these dominant seventh chords gives a blues sound. See the 12-bar blues progression on page 36.

RELATING THE GUITAR FINGERBOARD TO THE PIANO KEYBOARD

The guitar fingerboard can be related to the piano keyboard by thinking of the natural notes as white keys and the sharps and flats as black keys. The white keys on the piano make up a major scale (we know it as the C major scale) while the black keys are the half steps in between (the sharps and flats). Taken together, the five black keys on the piano, or the spaces between the major scale steps, make up a pentatonic scale (F♯ major pentatonic, to be exact). So, here you have white circles on the fingerboard as the notes of the major scale, and black circles as the notes of the pentatonic scale. Notice that the pentatonic rows are the exact reverse of the major rows, except that the major scale has two extra straight rows. (This diagram is in a C position, with the C major scale in white and the F♯ pentatonic in black.)

Fig. 33: F♯ Major Pentatonic (black) and

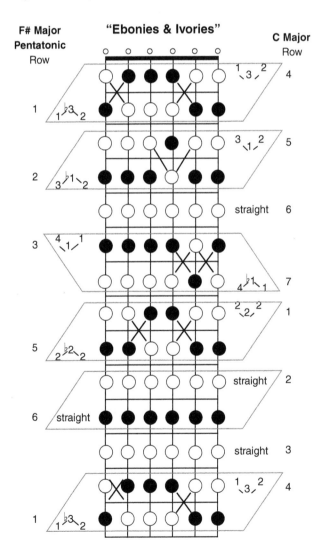

THE BLUES SCALE

There are many different descriptions of what comprises a "blues scale." The *blues scale* is basically a minor pentatonic scale (a pentatonic scale based on the sixth step of the major pentatonic scale) with added notes. Below is the minor pentatonic scale with additional notes in parentheses that may be added. They are written with all fingered notes even though you may play some of the intervals as bends.

Try creating these four versions of a blues scale by:

1. Adding the flatted fifth (to the minor pentatonic)
2. Adding the second, flatted fifth, and natural seventh
3. Adding the second and natural seventh
4. Adding the flatted fifth and natural seventh

NOTE:
The steps are numbered from A as "1." The rows of the A minor pentatonic scale are indicated, and the extra notes added fall outside the rows.

Fig. 34: A Blues Scale

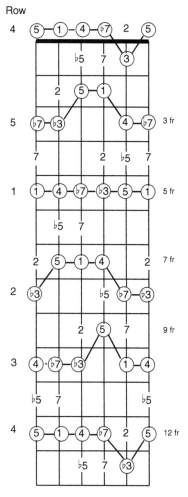

BLUES SCALE FINGERINGS

Here are some fingerings for blues scale #1 in G, in various positions. Of course, you can transpose to other keys by starting on a different fret. This blues scale adds the ♭5 to the minor pentatonic scale. So, the formula is 1–♭3–4–♭5–5–♭7. These are written with all fingered notes, although you may play some as bends.

Fig. 35: Blues Scale, Seven Fingerings in G

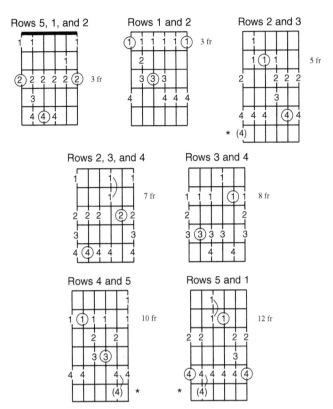

*Use the first-finger stretch going up and the fourth-finger stretch going down (always pulling back to position).

Next, let's look at some fingerings for blues scale #2 in G, in various positions. Of course, you can transpose to other keys by starting on a different fret. This blues scale adds three notes: the 2, ♭5, and 7, to the minor pentatonic scale. So, the formula is 1–2–♭3–4– ♭5–5–♭7–7. These are written with all fingered notes, although you may play some as bends.

Fig. 36: Blues Scale Variation, Seven Fingerings in G

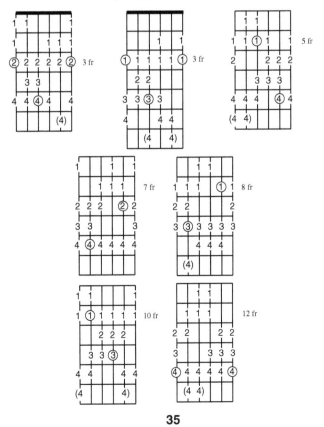

Play the scales given on the previous page against these common blues progressions:

Fig. 37A: 12-Bar Blues Progression in G

Fig. 37B: 12-Bar Blues Progression (Variation) in G

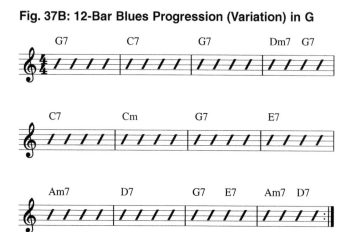

THE MODES

Using modes in your playing is simply a matter of deciding what scale to play against a given chord progression or bass line. In most Western music, we play in either Ionian or Aeolian modes (major or minor). However, playing in the other modes can give the music an interesting flavor. If you are playing a C major scale against a D chord progression (or beginning and ending on a D note), you would be playing in D Dorian. Below are the names of the modes, according to the scale degree that you begin upon.

By beginning and ending on the lowest note in each position, you can get the sound of each mode. You can play the scale in any position, simply by starting and ending with the degree of the scale pertaining to each mode.

1. Ionian (major scale)—start with scale degree 1
2. Dorian—start with scale degree 2
3. Phrygian—start with scale degree 3
4. Lydian—start with scale degree 4
5. Mixolydian—start with scale degree 5
6. Aeolian (natural minor scale)—start with scale degree 6
7. Locrian—start with scale degree 7

Fig. 38: C Major Scale, Degrees Across Fingerboard

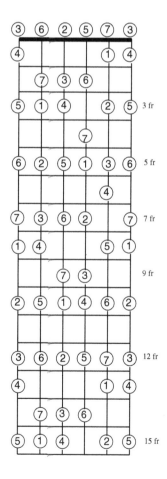

Here are some scale positions for the modes. The first degree of the scale is circled. Try them starting and ending on the first degree (root).

Fig. 39: Modes in the Keys of D and G

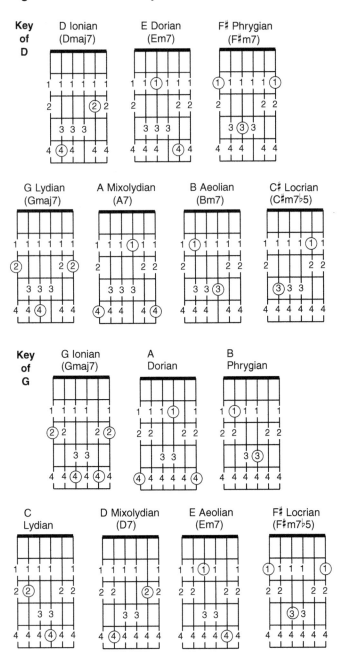

Here are some progressions that work well with various modes.

Dorian

Try improvising using notes from D Dorian. Remember that the D Dorian contains the same notes as the C major scale.

Fig. 40: Chord Progressions for D Dorian

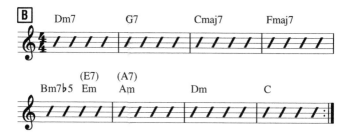

Phrygian

Try improvising using notes from E Phrygian (same notes as C major). Play the same progression using an E major chord instead of an E minor chord. This makes the "I" chord major and is the basis for much Spanish flamenco music.

Fig. 41: Chord Progressions for E Phrygian

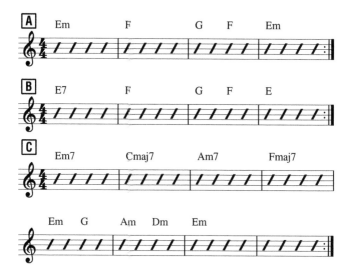

Lydian

Try improvising using notes from F Lydian (same notes as C major).

Fig. 42: Chord Progression for F Lydian

Mixolydian

Try improvising using notes from G Mixolydian (same notes as C major).

Fig. 43: Chord Progression for G Mixolydian

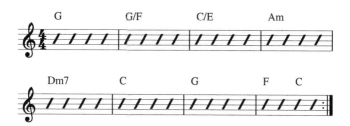

As we mentioned earlier, the *natural minor scale* is simply one of the modes of the major scale, starting on the sixth degree of the scale.

Notice that the first row of the minor scale corresponds exactly to the sixth row of the relative major scale.

Fig. 44: F Natural Minor Scale (or Aeolian Mode) and Its Relative Major

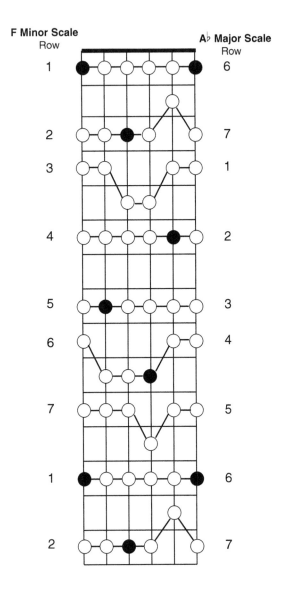

The *harmonic minor scale* is a common alteration of the natural minor scale. Simply raise the seventh degree one half step, or one fret. This "leading tone" brings the scale strongly back to the root and makes the V chord (built on C in the key of F minor) a dominant seventh, as in the major scale. Let's see how the rows look now:

Fig. 45: F Harmonic Minor Scale

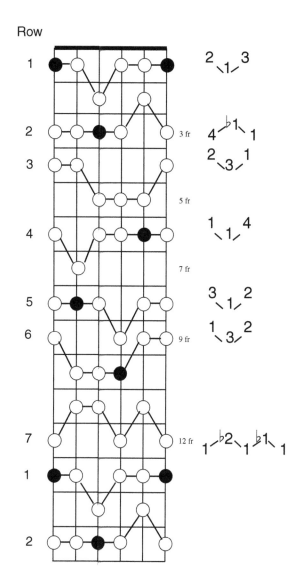

CHORDS DERIVED FROM THE HARMONIC MINOR SCALE

Each row contains one of the prime chords in F harmonic minor. Notice the more exotic seventh chords derived from this scale. These are typical jazz chord fingerings muting the first and fifth strings.

Fig. 46: F Harmonic Minor Scale, with Corresponding Chords

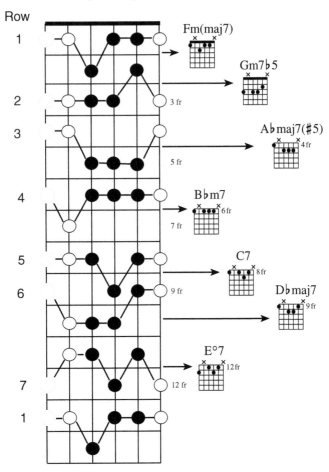

Here are seven fingerings for the harmonic minor scale, based on each row (on each scale step).

Fig. 47: Harmonic Minor Scale Fingerings

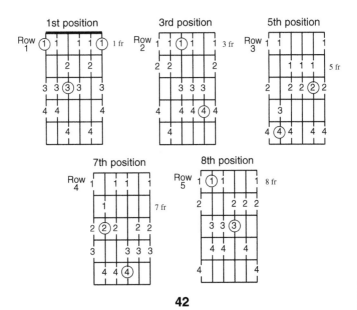

42

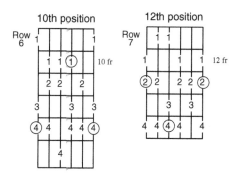

To include all 12 positions, here are five alternate fingerings for the harmonic minor scale.

Fig. 48: More Harmonic Minor Scale Fingerings

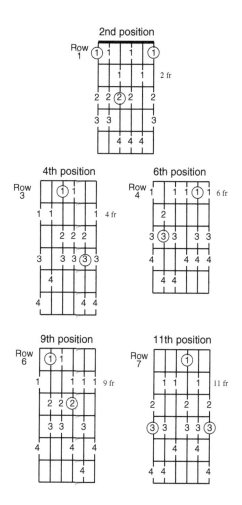

MODES OF THE HARMONIC MINOR SCALE

You can use different modes of the harmonic minor scale, just as the major scale. For instance, play an F harmonic minor scale starting on the fifth against a C7 chord. This would give you a C scale with a ♭2, ♭6, and ♭7 (a Mixolydian mode of the harmonic minor scale). This leads beautifully into the Fm chord (iv minor).

THE MELODIC MINOR SCALE

The *melodic minor scale* is another alteration of the natural minor scale. Simply raise both the sixth and seventh degree one half step, or one fret. This sounds almost like a cross between a major and minor scale. A common technique in classical music is to ascend with a melodic minor scale and to descend with a natural minor scale.

Let's examine our rows:

Fig. 49: F Melodic Minor Scale

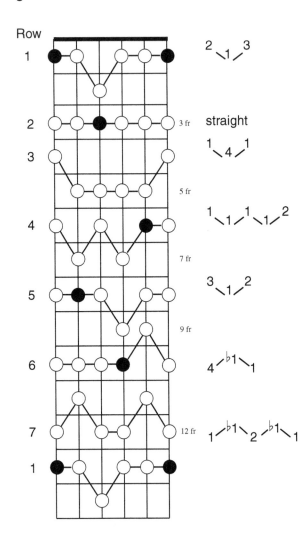

CHORDS DERIVED FROM THE MELODIC MINOR SCALE

Each row contains one of the prime chords of F melodic minor. Notice the two dominant seventh chords on B♭ and C. These are typical jazz chord forms, muting the first and fifth strings.

Fig. 50: Seventh Chords Within F Melodic Minor

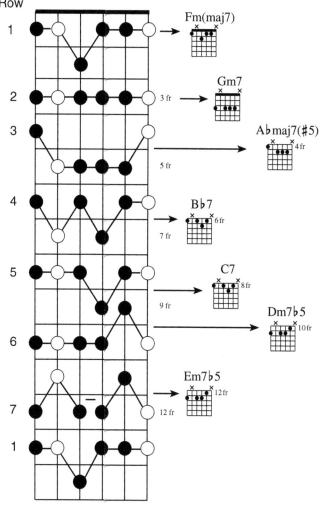

Here are some different fingerings for the melodic minor scale.

Fig. 51: Melodic Minor Scale Fingerings

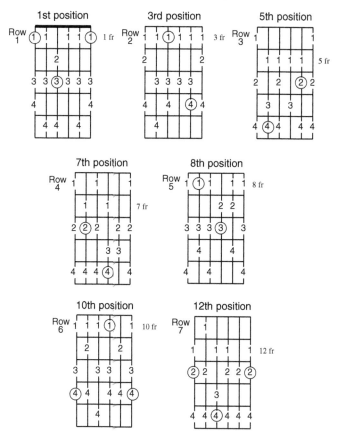

Here are alternate fingerings for the melodic minor scale, to include all 12 positions.

Fig. 52: More Melodic Minor Scale Fingerings

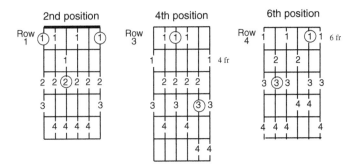

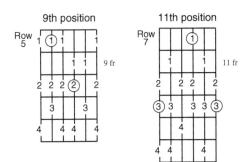

MODES OF THE MELODIC MINOR SCALE

You can use different modes of the melodic minor scale, just as in the major scale. For instance, play an F melodic minor scale against a C chord. This would give you a C scale with a ♭6 and ♭7 (a Mixolydian mode of the melodic minor scale). This scale starts out major and ends up minor, the reverse of the melodic minor. It's a nice temporary color, or leads beautifully into a iv chord, Fm, or a ii7♭5 chord, Dm7♭5.

THE WHOLE TONE SCALE

A *whole tone scale* has the same distance between each note: a whole step, or two frets. Therefore, you will find that all of the rows are exactly the same. Notice that the chords extracted from the rows are augmented chords.

Fig. 53: Whole Tone Scale

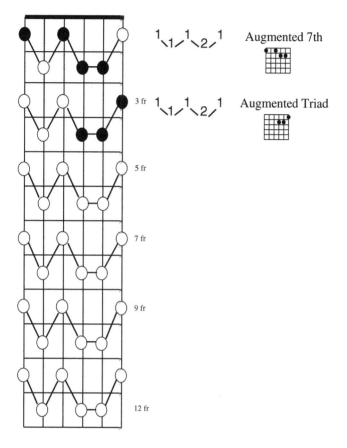

Augmented 7th

Augmented Triad

Here are some different ways to finger whole tone scales.

Figs. 54 : Whole Tone Scale (One Position)

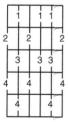
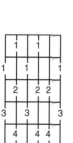
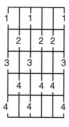

47

Figs. 55 : Whole Tone Scale (Position Shifting)

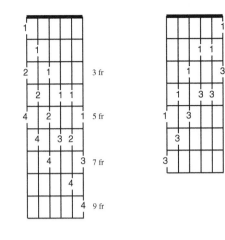

THE DIMINISHED SCALE

A *diminished scale* is an eight-note scale composed of alternating half steps and whole steps. This symmetrical pattern makes only two rows that repeat for the entire fingerboard. You can visualize these rows in two ways. In the diagram below, both rows contain typical diminished seventh chord shapes.

Fig. 56: Diminished Scale

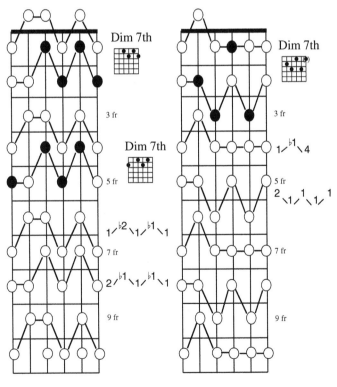

NOTE:
The diminished chord can be named for any of the four notes of the chord.

Here are some different ways to finger diminished scales. Playing three notes per string shifts the position back one fret (as in the first diagram). To go straight across the fingerboard, we need to play four notes on one string. As a result, we include one extra note beyond the three rows.

Try also continuing the same patterns across different sets of strings.

Fig. 57: Diminished Scale Fingerings

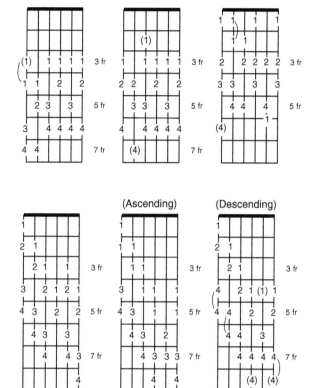

(Ascending)   (Descending)

Fig. 58: Open-Position Diminished Scale Fingerings

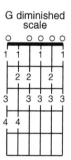

G diminished scale   F# diminished scale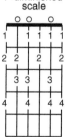

F diminished scale

When ascending, reach out one fret with the first finger and shift up back to position. When descending, extend one fret with the fourth finger and slide down back to position. Or, by playing four notes per string you will shift diagonally across the fingerboard.

Fig. 59: Chromatic Scale

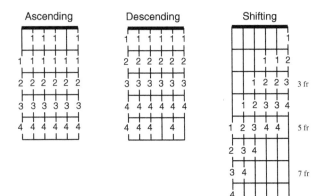

USING CHROMATICISM

You can include chromatic steps in other scales. Here is a major scale including some extra half steps, with suggested ways to reach and pull back into position. These are just examples; try other half steps.

Fig. 60: Major Scale with Added Chromatics

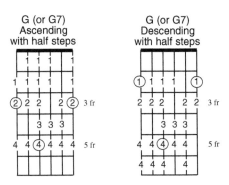

SEQUENTIAL FINGERINGS

One effective technique is to repeat a melodic figure on different sets of strings. You can play the same figure in three successive octaves by playing a pattern on the fifth and sixth strings, the same pattern two frets higher on the fourth and third strings, and then three frets higher on the second and first strings. For example, here are notes from an F major pentatonic scale in sequential octaves, fingered several ways. Find your own patterns starting from the other steps of the scale.

Fig. 61: F Major Pentatonic Scale (Sequenced with two fingerings)

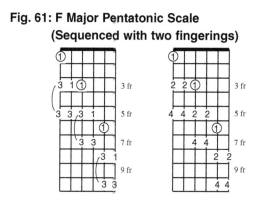

Fig. 62: F Major Pentatonic Scale (Sequenced beginning on second degree of scale)

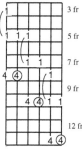

Fig. 63: F Major Pentatonic Scale (Sequenced beginning on third degree of scale)

Fig. 64: F Major Pentatonic Scale (Sequenced beginning on the fifth scale degree)

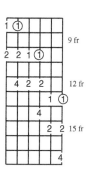
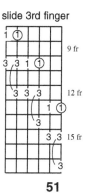
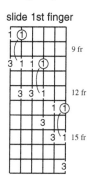

HARP-STYLE SCALES

By fingering two notes of a scale on two different strings whenever possible, and using open strings as often as possible, you can create scales with a harp-like effect. Let the notes of the scale ring into each other as much as possible. For ease of reading, the scales are written here in tablature.

Fig. 65: Harp Scales

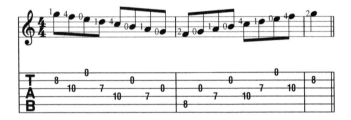

CIRCLE OF FIFTHS

Much of our music is structured around the interval of a perfect fifth. The naturally vibrating string sounds an octave higher when you produce an harmonic at the halfway point of the string (the twelfth fret), and it vibrates another perfect fifth higher when you produce a harmonic at the 1/3 point of the string (the seventh fret). So, it stands to reason that besides the unison and octave, the interval of a fifth occurs most easily in nature. To demonstrate just how many ways we use this interval in the structure of our music, let's arrange the notes in a circle, each one a perfect fifth apart from the last. This is called the "circle of fifths."

Fig. 66: Circle of Fifths

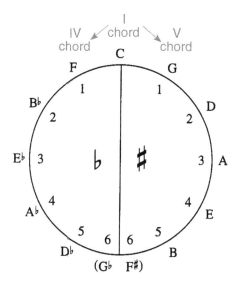

You can begin anywhere in the circle. By making each note into a seventh chord, you can play a progression moving counterclockwise, each chord resolving to the next: D7–G7–C7–F7–B♭7 etc. Musicians refer to this as "Going around the circle of fifths" (or the circle of fourths). Going around the other way is called *retrograde.*

We can use this diagram to find the sharps and flats that occur in each key. The number inside the circle indicates the number of sharps or flats in the major key just outside the circle. Notice that the number of sharps increases as you go around the circle clockwise, and the number of flats increases as you go around counterclockwise. The "order of sharps" begins with F# and moves clockwise, and flats begin with B♭ and move counterclockwise. For example, the key with three sharps (key of A major) will have the first three in the "order of sharps": F♯, C♯, and G♯. The key with two flats (B♭ major) will have the first two flats in the "order of flats": B♭ and E♭.

53

IMPROVISING OVER PROGRESSIONS

When improvising a melody, applying the right scale to a chord progression is not as hard as it might seem. We introduce the concept of "chord-scales" here as a quick way to see the relationship of the melody to the harmony. Chords are typically built up in thirds: 1, 3, 5, and 7. As extended harmonies are added (ninths, elevenths, thirteenths), the chord comes to include virtually all of the notes of the scale. In this way, we can refer to the available notes for both the chord and the scale as the "chord-scale."

To visualize the available notes, we map out a chord-scale this way. The prime chord tones are written as open circles. These are also the most common points of rest in a melody. The other notes of the extended chord are written as filled-in notes. These are more often passing tones and can also be more colorful resting points in a melody. A note written as an "x" can be a passing tone, but is likely to clash against the chord. The chord-scale also defines the notes you can use to build more extended chords in the accompaniment.

Fig. 67: Chord-Scales (Key of C)

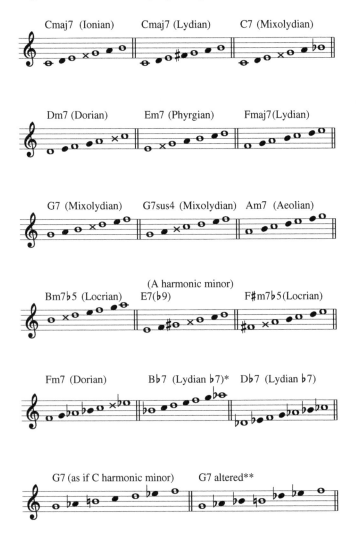

* Using an E♭ instead of an E here would result in a Mixolydian mode.
** Notice that G7 altered contains the same pitches as D♭7 Lydian.

Chord-scales can be constructed in different ways, depending upon the context. For example, the Em7 chord is a iii chord in the key of C, calling for a Phrygian mode. The Em7 is also a ii chord in the key of D, calling for a Dorian mode.

In the diagrams below, the chord-scales are shown on the top staff, with an example of an improvisation using that chord scale on the bottom staff.

Fig. 68: Sample Improvisations
(Using Chord-Scales as a Guide)

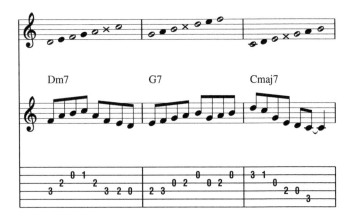

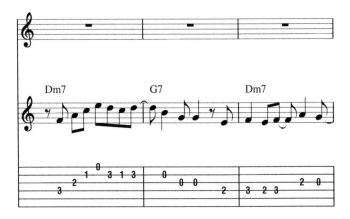

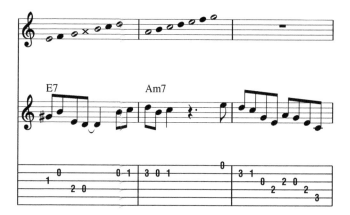

57

You can also use one scale throughout a progression. For example, try using a C major scale over the progression C–G–Am–Em–F–C–F–G–C. (While on the C chord, avoid the F note, but while on the F chord, you can accent the F note.) Then use the C7 chord-scale on the first (bluesy) progression below. Chord-scales and example improvisations are indicated below.

Fig. 69: Sample Improvisations (Using One Scale Throughout Entire Progression)

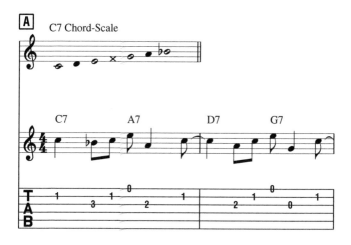

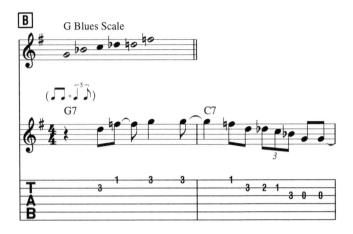

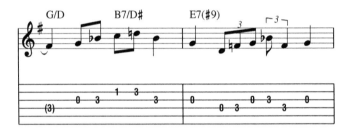

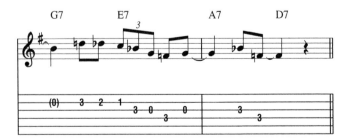

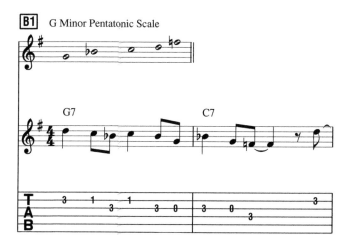

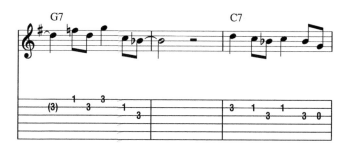

RIFFS OVER CHORD CHANGES

Here is a way to get started improvising scales over chord changes. Improvising doesn't necessarily mean a constant flow of new ideas; in a long melody there are often several motifs, or short phrases, that will be repeated.

An easy way to start to practice improvising over chord changes is to take one or two riffs (motifs, or licks) and play them over several chords in a progression. You can play the same melodic and rhythmic shape transposed to fit different chords. Experiment to find a timing to match the accompaniment. Also, try coming in on different beats in the measure (in which case, you may need to vary the riff to make it fit). Also, try leaving extra space between the riffs.

Here are some examples of riffs over chord changes. The riff in Fig. 70 works with either major or minor chords, since there is no third degree of the scale in the riff.

Fig. 70A: Blues Riff

Now, try sequencing this motif over a four-measure progression.

Fig. 70B: Blues Riff (Sequenced)

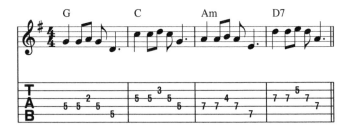

Here is a more complex one, with different riffs for major or minor chords.

Fig. 71A: Another Riff Idea

Once again, let's flesh this concept out over a full chord progression.

Fig. 71B: Another Riff Idea (Sequenced)

This one has a third riff—it works well over dominant seventh chords.

Fig. 72A: Seventh Chord Riff

Now, try over a full chord progression.

Fig. 72B: Seventh Chord Riff (Sequenced)

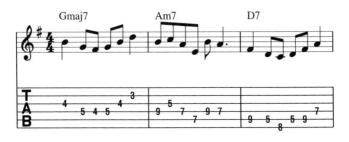

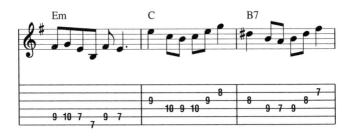

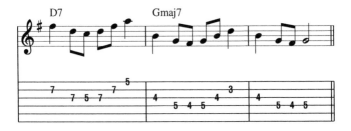

Here are three different riffs to play over the same chord changes. Make up your own, starting with a simple two- or three-note phrase that you can play with ease. The most important part of improvising is to keep the rhythm going.

Fig. 73A: More Seventh Chord Riffs

And finally, here are the riffs sequenced over a full chord progression.

Fig. 73B: More Seventh Chord Riffs (Sequenced)

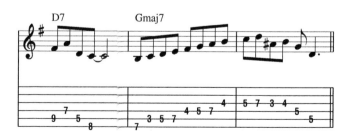

ALTERNATE TUNINGS

Many players use alternate tunings which are designed to facilitate certain scales or chords.

DADGAD TUNING

DADGAD contains three D notes, and in fact, the open strings are the 1, 4, and 5 of the D scale (major or minor). Here is the D major scale diagramed in D–A–D–G–A–D tuning.

Fig. 74: D Major Scale (DADGAD Tuning)

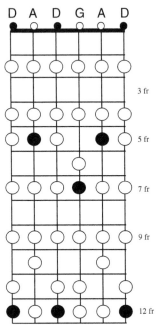

OPEN E TUNING

Open E contains the notes of the E major chord (1, 3, and 5). Here is the E major scale in E–B–E–G♯–B–E tuning.

Fig. 75: E Major Scale (Open E Tuning)

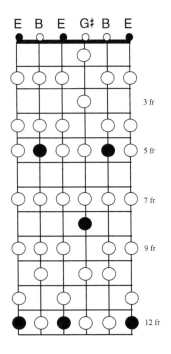

DROP D TUNING

In *Drop D*, because the sixth string is tuned one whole step lower than standard (from E down to D), you need to finger the notes on that string two frets higher to compensate. Here is the D major scale in D–A–D–G–B–E tuning.

Fig. 76: D Major Scale (Drop D Tuning)

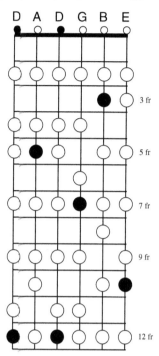

DROP G TUNING

In *Drop G*, because the sixth and fifth strings are tuned one whole step lower than standard (from E and A down to D and G respectively, you need to finger the notes on those strings two frets higher to compensate. Here is the G major scale in D–G–D–G–B–E tuning.

Fig. 77: G Major Scale (Drop G Tuning)

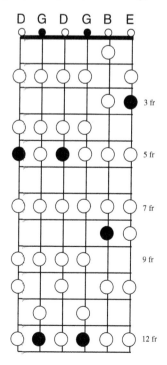

OPEN G TUNING

Open G (with the first string also dropped down to a D) also moves the notes up two frets on the first string. Here is the G major scale in D–G–D–G–B–D tuning.

Fig. 78: G Major Scale (Open G Tuning)

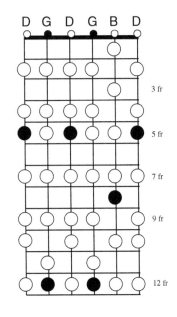

TUNING IN FOURTHS

Tuning the guitar completely in fourths creates very consistent patterns for scales. Because all the intervals between the strings remain the same, all scale patterns will be consistent when moving from one set of strings to the next! Here is the F major scale in E–A–D–G–C–F tuning. Notice the diagonal lines that leap out! To visualize patterns with this tuning system throughout the book, imagine cutting all the scale diagrams between the second and third strings, and shifting the right side up the distance of one fret.

Fig. 79: F Major Scale (E–A–D–G–C–F Tuning)

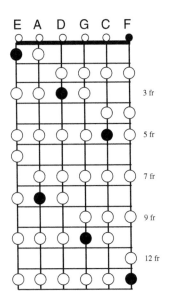

COMPOSITE SCALES

A *tetrachord* is a succession of four notes. You can create scales, including some fairly exotic ones, by combining two tetrachords. Divide a fourth into any order of whole steps and half steps, and you'll have a tetrachord. Put any two tetrachords together, and see what you get. Usually the tetrachords may be separated by a whole or half step, the lower tetrachord starting on the root and the upper tetrachord starting on the fifth. However, a tetrachord that spans an augmented fourth can use the same note for the top of the first tetrachord and the bottom of the second tetrachord.

Here are some tetrachords found in common scales:

Fig. 80: Tetrachords

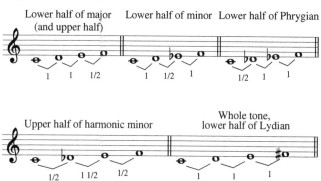

Here are other possible tetrachords:

Fig. 81: More Tetrachords

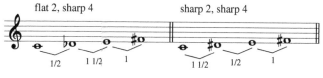

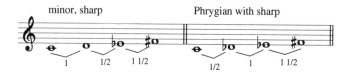

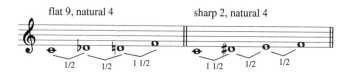

Here are some different combinations of tetrachords that result in scales. The most common is the major scale. Yet, you can build many more exotic scales.

Fig. 82: Tetrachords Within the Major Scale & Melodic Minor Scale

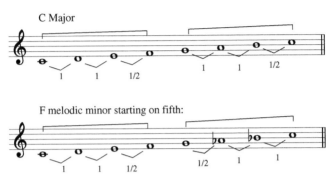

Here are some less ordinary combinations:

Fig. 83: Tetrachords Within More Exotic Scales

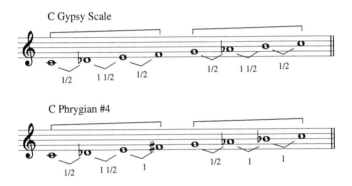

This one combines diminished and whole-tone tetrachords.

Fig. 84: Tetrachords Within the Altered Dominant Scale

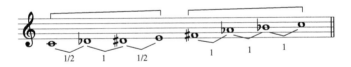

MOVEABLE SCALE FINDER

This is a way to more easily visualize transposing to any of the twelve keys from one diagram. First, photocopy this page (you'll want to be able to use it more than just once). Write out any scale you'd like to transpose in the diagram on the left. To the right is the Scale Finder—the letters along the left side of the Scale Finder show the names of the notes along the guitar's sixth string. To transpose your original diagram, just find the appropriate sixth-string root on the Scale Finder, and then rewrite the scale pattern beginning there, starting with your first row. If you like, you can actually cut out the Scale Finder and overlay it on top of your original diagram. Slide it until the root of the original scale lines up with the new root on your Scale Finder; that will be the position for the new key.

Remember: Rows repeat themselves at the twelfth fret, so anything that appears beyond the twelfth fret also occurs in open position.

Fig. 85: Moveable Scale Finder

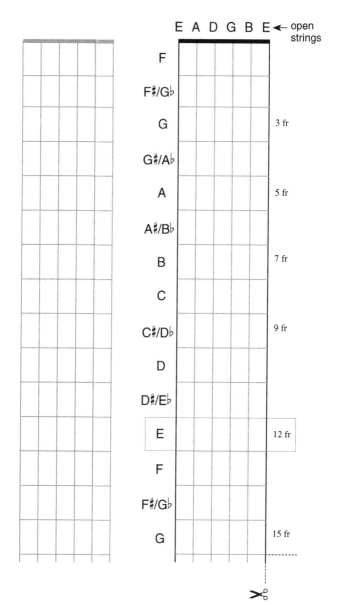

ABOUT THE AUTHORS

Noted guitarist, composer, and educator Jim Scott has taught his unique system of "rows" in workshops throughout the country. As a member of the Paul Winter Consort, he was co-composer of "Missa Gaia/Earth Mass" and the familiar voice on the song "Common Ground." He has produced several recordings of original music and written numerous choral compositions, a stage musical, and a music video for children. Info on Jim can be found at *www.jimscottsongs.com.*

Muriel Anderson is a winner of the National Fingerpicking Guitar Championship and has authored several books including *All Chords in All Positions, Building Guitar Arrangements from the Ground Up,* as well as several books of her original music and transcriptions. She is the founder/producer of "Muriel Anderson's All-Star Guitar Night." In addition to maintaining a vigorous concert schedule, she also teaches guitar at Belmont University in Nashville. Muriel has released three videos and six CDs, available at Tower Records, Borders Books, 1-800-BUY-MYCD, or *www.murielanderson.com.*